PAUL
RABBI
AND
APOSTLE

PAUL

RABBI

AND

APOSTLE

Pinchas Lapide/Peter Stuhlmacher

Translated by Lawrence W. Denef

AUGSBURG Publishing House • Minneapolis

PAUL: RABBI AND APOSTLE

English language edition copyright © 1984 Augsburg Publishing House

Original German edition entitled *Paulus: Rabbi und Apostel,* copyright © 1981 Calwer Verlag, Stuttgart, and Kösel-Verlag GmbH & Co., Munich.

Scripture quotations unless otherwise noted are from the Revised Standard Version of the Bible, copyright 1946, 1952, and 1971 by the Division of Christian Education of the National Council of Churches.

Library of Congress Cataloging in Publication Data

Lapide, Pinchas, 1922-
   PAUL: RABBI AND APOSTLE.

   Translation of: Paulus, Rabbi und Apostel.
   Bibliography: p.
   1. Paul, the Apostle, Saint—Addresses, essays,
lectures. I. Stuhlmacher, Peter. II. Title.
BS2506.L3613   1984   225.9'24   84-24382
ISBN 0-8066-2122-2 (pbk.)

Manufactured in the U.S.A.   APH 10-4903

1 2 3 4 5 6 7 8 9 0 1 2 3 4 5 6 7 8 9

CONTENTS

PREFACE

To observe recent Jewish-Christian dialogue is to note that things are on the move. In church academies and in schools of higher education an attempt is being made to reappraise and overcome the painful memories of opposition in the past. In the process it seems that a rather recent event—the Holocaust—has become the common point of reference. Its lasting effects can be detected everywhere. That we can learn from it and that we ought to learn from it is indisputable. The history that led to the Holocaust must never be forgotten or repressed. This history, however, dare not be confined only to intellectual and emotional realms. Above all, it must find its way from the halls of scholarship to the general public. How to accomplish this should be a task for all of us, primarily for Christians, whose very lives have been shaped by the existence of the Jewish people. The current investigation of Jewish history and the roots of anti-Semitism are essential and relevant, and dare not be neglected. But even more pressing are those questions concerning the place of reconciliation and the source of its forgiving and unifying power. The strength for reconciliation does not come from within, from our efforts and accomplishments, but from God's mercy. God has manifested his mercy toward us in Jesus Christ; that is a Christian confession our Jewish faith brothers and sisters cannot accept. But, for the sake of truth it simply must be acknowledged that although we mutually respect one another's boundaries, this does not mean that there are no border crossings in approaching one another. A small beginning could become a large "border traffic," not only for geographic, economic, and political topics, but more significantly, religious concerns.

A modest beginning has been made in places where Christian congregations examine and seek to understand Jewish beliefs, Old Testament ethics, and contemporary synagogue worship, where people pray for and with one another that God's presence and reconciliation might be experienced and his kingdom come, and where social questions again become genuine questions for faith.

In this spirit an interreligious dialogue between Professor Pinchas Lapide and Professor Peter Stuhlmacher was conducted at a conference of pastors and theologians of the regional church of Pforzheim. The results of their dialogue on the theme, "Paul: Rabbi and Apostle," are contained in this book and can perhaps be most briefly summarized as follows: Although, or better yet, because, Paul sees in Christ the "new creation," he never tires of proclaiming "peace and mercy" on all his believers, as well as on "the Israel of God" (Gal. 6:15f.).

FRITZ ALLGEIER

PAUL:
APOSTATE OR APOSTLE?

Peter Stuhlmacher

It is uniquely gratifying when Jews and Christians enter into serious fraternal dialogue about the fundamentals of their faith and by this dialogue endeavor to understand one another in their commonalities and differences. The Jewish-Christian theological conversation which has been stimulated in recent years by Dr. Pinchas Lapide in a way for which we can be thankful has already taken up problems of an essential nature. Among them have been belief in the resurrection,[1] the understanding of God in Judaism and Christianity,[2] and the person and work of Jesus of Nazareth.[3] I consider it especially noteworthy that during the course of the various discussions thus far Professor Lapide has never called on the Christian side to relinquish any articles of faith that indicate the direction for the Chris-

tian way of faith. Rather, on the basis of the Old Testament-Jewish tradition, he has furnished his Christian
partners with new and better insights into their own
tradition, while at the same time formulating those spe-
cifically Jewish questions we Christians need to hear.
In the meanwhile this openness of Lapide toward the
Christian tradition has been seriously criticized from
the Jewish side, and he has been accused of seeking
Jewish-Christian agreement at the expense of the con-
victions of his Jewish comrades.[4] I sincerely hope that
despite this critique, which in my opinion is unfounded,
we can engage in a discussion of Paul that will add
to our mutual understanding. The truth of faith dis-
closes itself to both Jews and Christians who open their
hearts and minds to it. It denies itself, however, to those
who seek to use it as a "means of achieving their own
ends." And the truth of faith withdraws itself entirely
from those who by means of this truth want to be
absolutely and always in the right. The theme proposed
by Pinchas Lapide, "Paul: Apostate or Apostle?," was
the topic for a Jewish-Christian dialogue already held
in 1976 in Munich.[5] It is worthy of mutual consideration again.

1. A Point of Departure for a New Dialogue

In the face of everything that historically connects
and separates Jews and Christians, I think it is advis-
able to begin by responding historically to the question
posed by our theme, and to do so as accurately as possible. Since we are dealing with Paul we ought first of

all speak about the historical character of the apostle, his work, and his proclamation of the gospel which was controversial from the very beginning. For the moment, we should set aside the multitude of Jewish and Christian interpretations of Paul.

It is well known that Paul can be understood in many different ways. He can be portrayed as the principal witness to the one true gospel in the New Testament. Paul can also be seen as an apostolic outsider and so as the one actually responsible for the irrevocable breach between the synagogue and Christian community. He can be viewed as the first pioneering theologian of mission-oriented Hellenistic Christianity. His theology and proclamation can also be interpreted, however, as arising entirely out of Jewish roots. Therefore before we enter into the argument as to just how Paul is to be understood today, we must closely examine the historical facts and traditions, accessible to all of us. Only when we have these facts before us—and not before— can we engage in an appropriate interpretation of Paul.

2. The Available Historical Facts

The external historical facts for the life and work of Paul are to be ascertained from the book of Acts and the letters of Paul taken together.[6] They can be enumerated rather quickly. Paul comes from Tarsus in Cilicia (Acts 22:3), and from a pious Jewish family. In accordance with custom he was circumcised on the eighth day (Phil. 3:5) and brought up in the ancient

religious traditions. Some time after his birth, according to Acts 22:3 and 26:4, his family moved to Jerusalem. There, in the Jerusalem school of Rabban Gam-
aliel I, Paul was educated as a scribe (Acts 22:3).
Evidences of this training are still recognizable in the
typical rabbinic arguments and interpretations of Holy
Scripture that run through Paul's writings. In Phil. 3:5
Paul refers to himself as a Pharisee who is faithful to
the law. In Gal. 1:14 he relates that he was more advanced in Judaism than many of his own age and
fellow believers, and that he was "extremely zealous"
for the traditions of the fathers.

Taking these factors into account we can say with
some certainty that Paul was a strict "scribe of the
Pharisees" (Mark 2:16) who arose out of the Jewish
diaspora. His first contact with the Christian faith took
place a short time after Jesus' crucifixion in Jerusalem.
At that time the preaching of Christ by Stephen and his
friends had enraged the Greek-speaking Jews in Jerusalem. Finding Stephen's critique of the Jerusalem temple and of the Law of Sinai—spoken in the name of
Jesus (Acts 6:14)—blasphemous, these diaspora Jews,
who had returned to Jerusalem for religious reasons,
took the law into their own hands, stoned Stephen, and
saw to it that his followers were driven out of Jerusalem
(Acts 7:54—8:3).[7] Paul was a witness of these events
and joined in defending the Jewish faith against the
Christian apostates (Acts 8:1-3; Gal. 1:13; 1 Cor.
15:9).

Seeing that the preaching of the Stephen circle, which

had been expelled from Jerusalem, also began to attract adherents from the large community of diaspora Jews in Damascus, Paul requested letters of recommendation from the highest Jewish court in Jerusalem, and set out to stir up the synagogues in Damascus against the new faith in Christ (Acts 9:1f.; 22:19; 26:12). The primary means available to the synagogues for punishing apostate members were public flogging and expulsion from the community.

Paul's persecution of Christians in Damascus, however, never took place. On his way to the city Paul was surprised by an appearance of Christ. For the remainder of his life Paul considered this appearance equivalent to the commissioning appearances of Jesus to Peter and the other apostles. It convinced him, the fanatic Pharisee, that the Christian faith he had previously persecuted was true before God and the only way to God. On the other hand, his combative zeal for the law came to be seen as a struggle against God's revelation in the person of the crucified and resurrected Messiah, Jesus (Gal. 1:13-16; 1 Cor. 15:8-10; 2 Cor. 5:16-17; Phil. 3:2-11). Paul spontaneously entered into the service of the Lord he had previously persecuted (Acts 9:4f.) and became an "apostle" (ambassador) and "servant of Jesus Christ" (Rom. 1:1).

The consequences of Paul's mission work on behalf of Christ among the synagogue congregations were immediate. Now it was he who was repeatedly flogged as an enemy of the law[8] and once (according to Acts 14:19 in Lystra) almost stoned to death. In addition

he was on numerous occasions sentenced to beatings by
Roman authorities, more than likely for disturbing the
peace. In 2 Cor. 11:24f. Paul summarizes: "Five times
I have received at the hands of the Jews the forty lashes
less one. Three times I have been beaten with rods;
once I was stoned. . . ." In other words, during the
course of his mission Paul incurred the very same
punishments that as a militant Pharisee he had intended for the colleagues of Stephen (Acts 22:19), and
under which he had seen Stephen die in Jerusalem. The
sharp tone that recurs in Paul's letters, for example,
the unfortunately formulated polemic in 1 Thess. 2:14f.,
can, in my opinion, be explained as a direct result of
this situation of personal conflict and suffering.

After Paul had conducted his mission alone for some
time (Gal. 1:18 and 2:1 imply that it was about 10
years), Barnabas brought him to Antioch (Acts 11:25f.).
Antioch meanwhile had become the assembly point for
the members of the Stephen circle who had been driven
out of Jerusalem, and consequently had arisen as the
pioneering center for mission to the Gentiles (Acts
11:19-26). At first Paul conducted his mission to the
Gentiles from Antioch with Barnabas, but after the so-
called Apostolic Council he worked on his own authority. He considered this mission to the Gentiles his
special life's work for which he had been set aside by
God in Christ (Rom. 1:5). In carrying out this mission
the requirements of circumcision and obedience to all
613 commands and prohibitions of the Mosaic law
were consciously waived. It was precisely this renuncia-

tion that at first aroused suspicion and then a determined opposition to the venture of the Antiochians
and Paul, not only by faithful Jews, but also by those
Jewish Christians who had remained within the community of Israel. The issue was already a topic for
debate at the Apostolic Council (Gal. 2:1-10; Acts 15).
And the book of Acts goes on to indicate that there
were clashes with the Jews in every city that Paul
entered on his missionary journeys. The letter to the
Galatians and Rom. 15:30f. amplify this rather sche-
matic portrayal. Not only the Jews of the synagogues,
but also the wing of Jewish Christianity oriented to
James and Jerusalem who had remained faithful to the
law, remained openly skeptical of Paul and his mission
work. When, during his last visit to Jerusalem, the
apostle was seized in the temple, placed under custody,
and accused of taking a Gentile from Ephesus into the
inner court of the temple (Acts 21:27-36), the Christians of Jerusalem obviously did not stand up for him
in any special way.[9] He had to struggle through the
matter on his own. All historical traces of Paul in Rome
are lost, where he most likely was brought to trial
before Nero. Here too we hear nothing about support
from the Roman congregation.[10]

With these factual materials before us, we can make
an initial attempt to answer the question posed by our
theme. How ought we view Paul—as an apostate or as
an apostle of Jesus Christ? On the basis of the appearance of the risen Christ on the Damascus road, Paul
considered himself called to be an apostle of Jesus

Christ to the Gentiles, and dedicated his entire life to proclaiming the law-free gospel of Christ which had been revealed to him. However, it was precisely in his capacity as an apostle of Jesus Christ that Paul appeared as the betrayer of his ancestral faith; not only to the Pharisees who had once been his colleagues, and to many law-keeping Jews, but also to those Jewish Christians in Jerusalem and throughout the world through which he traveled, who continued to be devoted to "the traditions of the fathers" (Gal. 1:14). For them Paul was an apostate deserving condemnation, severe punishment, and if possible, even death (Acts 23:12ff.). The question posed by the theme before us will not allow a simple alternative answer.

3. Paul's Defense of His Gospel in the Letter to the Romans

In light of the complex nature of the question of Paul's identity, it is even more interesting to determine how Paul conducted himself in the battle that was forced on him and which arguments he used in his defense. In this regard his letters to the Galatians and Romans provide us with especially interesting information. Paul defended the legitimacy of his apostolate and with it the revelational quality of his gospel of Christ with great ardor and persistence (see Gal. 1:1-17 and Rom. 1:1-5). With the same intensity, however, he also countered the Jewish and Jewish-Christian accusation that in his proclamation of the gospel he had become unfaithful to the faith of Israel (Gal. 2:15; 4:21—5:1; 1 Cor. 9:19-23; Rom. 9–11). According to 1 Cor. 1:30 the essential content of the Pauline gospel is Jesus, the crucified and risen Messiah, "whom God made our wisdom, our righteousness and sanctification and redemption." According to Rom. 1:16 and the entire epistle to the Romans this gospel of Christ applies "to the Jew first and also to the Greek." As Messiah, Jesus became "a servant of the circumcision" in order to confirm God's faithfulness to the promises given to the patriarchs. It was only through an added act of grace that the Gentiles were accepted by God in Christ (Rom. 15:8f.).

In my opinion, Paul's letter to the Romans is not an abstract dialogue with presumed Jewish critics of Paul's preaching who have been introduced for merely rhetorical reasons. Even less should it be seen simply as a dogmatic compendium of Pauline doctrine in its purest expression. Rather, it is an apologetic development of the Pauline gospel in the face of accusations that were being spread about Paul in Rome.[11] The Jewish-Christian criticism of Paul's preaching of justification, which we find in Galatians, 2 Corinthians, and Philippians, was naturally also known in Rome, that is, even before Paul himself was able to visit the congregation. More than likely, those rumor-mongers who circulated this criticism like itinerant peddlers were members of the Petrine mission, and Roman believers sympathetic to Jewish Christianity in Jerusalem. If the Gentile Christians converted to the Christian faith in Rome were in-

deed largely "God-fearers" (that is, persons well-ac-
quainted with the Jewish faith tradition),[12] it is quite
understandable that and why the critics of Paul in Rome
found interested listeners. When we recognize that
Paul's letter to the Romans is just as situation oriented
as all of his other letters then we can, in reading it,
perceive how Paul tried by letter to defuse the criticism
against him being circulated in Rome and thereby open
up the way for the Gentile mission in the West.

The accusations of interest to us all have a Jewish-
Christian origin, and proceed rather like this: (1) In
comparison with the gospel of the original Jerusalem
apostles and the basic tenets of faith held by the Roman
congregation from its very beginning, the proclamation
of Paul appears to be an inappropriate innovation. (2)
Paul's gospel of justification smooths over the distinction that exists between Jews and Gentiles from the
perspective of the history of salvation. (3) Paul's criticism of the validity of the Mosaic law undermines
ethics and leads to moral arbitrariness. (4) Instead of
leading God's chosen people, Israel, to salvation, Paul's
mission has just the opposite effect: the Gentiles re-
spond favorably to the faith, whereas the Jews throughout the diaspora vehemently reject Paul's preaching of
Christ! The question before us, whether Paul is a legiti-
mate apostle or even an apostate, stands behind all
these accusations and makes Paul's counterargument
even more interesting.

From the very outset of this carefully thought
through letter, Paul undermines the first accusation by

explicitly declaring himself in complete agreement with the Jewish-Christian tradition of faith acknowledged by the Roman church. At the same time he continuously underscores the fact that his gospel is anchored in Holy Scripture. The thanksgiving of Rom. 6:17f. belongs in the context of this argument: "But thanks be to God, that you who were once slaves of sin have become obedient from the heart to the standard of teaching to which you were committed [by your missionaries], and, having been set free from sin, have become slaves of righteousness." Those in Rome who listen closely to the reading of the Roman letter, not only can but also should recognize that the early traditions concerning Christ cited by Paul (for example, Rom. 1:3f.; 3:25f.; or 4:25, among others) have been incorporated into the Pauline gospel and form its backbone: Christ is the messianic Son of God promised in the Scriptures. In his life and through his sacrificial death of atonement God himself has already established the eschatological day of reconciliation, albeit in a way that remains hidden. Like Abraham (see Gen. 22:1-19), God himself offered up his only Son as expiation for all believers, thereby revealing his world-sustaining love and righteousness (Rom. 8:31-39).

According to the sayings of the elders of Israel collected in the Mishnah, Tractate Aboth, what distinguishes the people of God from the Gentiles is that the will and the love of God the Creator have been made known to them directly in the revelation of the Torah on Sinai.[13] Paul in no way annuls this preferential status of Israel with his gospel. The gospel concerning the righteousness of God in Christ is meant for the Jews first and above all, and then also for the Greeks. By sending his Son, God affirmed his promise for Israel and as an addition, by sheer grace, also guaranteed the participation of the Gentiles in his coming kingly rule. According to Rom. 1:16f.; 2:9f.; 3:1f., 29f.; 9:1-5; 11:1ff.; and 15:8 there is no possibility of claiming that Paul has abandoned the history of salvation distinction between Jews and Gentiles and established his gospel of justification in direct opposition to the promises of Scripture. On the contrary, it is decisively important for the apostle that Jesus died on behalf of, not in condemnation of, Israel. According to Paul, the gospel would not be worthy of its designation as "the message of reconciliation" (2 Cor. 5:19) if Israel had forfeited reconciliation. Nor could it be the good news of God, who in Christ reconciled "the world" to himself, if the Gentiles would be excluded from the saving action of the atoning, sacrificial death of Jesus.

The third accusation—that to disqualify the law of Sinai as the embodiment of sin opens the door to un-bridled immorality under the guise of faith in Christ—Paul dismisses in Rom. 3:5-8, 31; 6:1ff.; and most forcefully in 7:7—8:11. Nonetheless, he expects his conversation partners and critics to follow precisely the same realization that had been made known to him by God in the vision of the resurrected Christ on the way to Damascus, and which had been inscribed indelibly on his conscience through this special revelation. For on this basis Paul knows that even the most radical passion for the Mosaic law cannot free one from enmity against God which is rooted in sin, but rather drives one ever deeper into it! Only Jesus' redemptive death is capable of saving us from this hostility toward God; therefore the law must be understood from the perspective of the death and resurrection of Jesus. In obedience to God, Jesus went to his death guiltless. To be sure, in the light of Deut. 21:23, his death on the cross seemed to be the curse of God upon a blasphemer and a transgressor of the law. Nevertheless, his resurrection and his exaltation to the right hand of God document the fact that God has affirmed Jesus' mission and vindicated him in the face of his judges and executioners. It is for this reason that the death of God's guiltless Son must be understood as a vicarious atoning sacrifice: Jesus has vicariously borne the curse of the law on behalf of sinners and purchased their freedom from bondage to the law, with his own life (Gal. 3:13; Rom. 8:3f.). From God's perspective and with Isaiah 53 in mind we can say: Jesus "was put to death [by God] for our trespasses and raised [by God] for our justification" (Rom. 4:25). Those Jews and Gentiles who acknowledge this saving act of God as occurring for them, and believe in Christ as their Lord and Advocate will be freed from the bondage of sin and regain access to the peace of God from which they have fallen and been excluded (Rom. 5:1-11). As a consequence, the law which denounces and condemns sin-

ners as such no longer holds any power over those who
have been reconciled to God through Christ.

As a consequence of his Damascus road encounter
with the risen Christ, Paul proclaimed Jesus Christ as
"the end of the law" for "everyone who has faith"
(Rom. 10:4), and at the same time as the Lord who
calls all into the service of righteousness and whose
Torah (Gal. 6:2) corresponds eschatologically to the
Torah of Sinai. Or, using the imagery of the fall in
Genesis 3, Paul can express this viewpoint in yet another way: In Christ, and on the basis of his sacrificial
death, the will of God is at last realized as it was
originally intended for Adam in Paradise, namely, as
the protection and direction for life in God's presence
—life lived out of love and in love (Rom. 8:1f.;
13:8f.). Paul himself was never an antinomian and
should therefore not be portrayed subsequently by others as one who despised the law. His criticism of the
Sinai Torah is a criticism which attempts to set free
and establish the original and eschatological will of God
that has been revealed in Christ and in his commandments! [14]

In Romans 9–11 Paul refutes the fourth and last accusation—that his proclamation of the gospel has led
to Israel's obstinacy rather than to its salvation—in a
very persuasive, and, if my perceptions are correct, once
again typically Jewish fashion. As already indicated,
he in no way denies Israel's preeminence in the history
of salvation. Instead he expressly underscores it at the
very beginning of these three impressive chapters. For

Paul, Israel remains God's chosen people who have been promised the coming of a messianic redeemer and participation in his kingly rule. Under this assumption, stated in Rom. 9:1-6 and again in Rom. 11:25-32 as the framework within which the apostle develops his entire argument, Paul conceives the mission to the Gentiles, for which he and others have been set apart, as a temporary interim phase on the historical way to the salvation of "all Israel" through faith in the Messiah Jesus. Paul interprets the election of Israel as an election to salvation through Christ by virtue of God's mercy. The rejection of his missionary gospel by the majority of Jews is a bitterly painful reality which he readily admits; but he understands it within the context of a boldly devised interpretation of salvation history that bears unmistakable apocalyptic features. When Paul and the other missionaries to the Gentiles have led "the full number of the Gentiles," as determined by God, to faith in Christ, the time of obstinacy toward the gospel of Christ imposed on Israel will come to an end. Then, in accordance with the irrevocable promise of God (Isa. 59:20f. and Jer. 31:33f.), Israel will be called to faith by the messianic Deliverer who will return from Zion. So Israel will also receive the forgiveness of her sins. However, the Deliverer who returns from Zion will be Jesus Christ. For God has consigned the Gentiles as well as the Jews to disbelief, precisely so that he might in Christ have mercy upon all (Rom. 11:25-32). Both Jews and Gentiles together make up the true eschatological people of God.[15] According to

Paul the goal of salvation history is the redemption of Israel through the Messiah Jesus and the gathering of the eschatological people of God. Before this goal is attained one cannot speak of the fulfillment of God's promises. Paul's intention as an apostle is not to oppose but to benefit Israel, since Christ, according to his understanding, has been sent, given over to death, and raised again, not against, but for Israel and for all the peoples of this world.

A short time after writing the letter to the Romans Paul was arrested in Jerusalem for having allegedly desecrated the temple, and, after a lengthy incarceration in Caesarea, brought to Rome as a Roman prisoner. It is no longer possible for us to determine whether the letter to the Romans had an ameliorating effect and silenced Paul's critics. Luke reports the arrival of Paul in the world capital with striking restraint. So Paul historically continues to be the highly controversial figure he already was in his own time, and as a result, the question posed by our theme remains historically open. Paul conceived of himself as having been commissioned by Jesus as an apostle to the Gentiles for Israel's sake. His Jewish and Jewish-Christian opponents, however, never ceased accusing him of apostasy, that is, of having departed from the traditional teachings of the elders of Israel.

4. Paul: Apostle to the Gentiles for Israel's Sake

The question whether Paul should be viewed as an apostle or as an apostate can thus be answered once we have taken into account the historical events and the continuing controversy surrounding Paul which we have just surveyed. It is a question of the life and work of the diaspora Pharisee, Paul, born in Tarsus of the lineage of Benjamin; it has been asked from the beginning of his ministry as an apostle and has from the beginning been answered in various ways.

When we take up the question anew today it seems to me that several factors should be considered. Historically it is beyond doubt that Paul worked as an apostle, and indeed more intensively and with greater lasting impact than all of the other apostles of Jesus whose names we know. Given these circumstances, it would be senseless for us to dispute Paul's historical role as an apostle. It is more meaningful to concentrate on the dialectical message of Paul and to enter into dialogue with him about the essential content of the Christian faith, particularly when we are involved in a fraternal conversation between Jews and Christians. But in such a conversation it is also historically pointless to deny that Paul was seen as an apostate by his fellow Jews and by many Jewish Christians and as such was persecuted and ostracized by them. Jesus had already awakened both faith and opposition among his Israelite contemporaries, and with Paul the process was repeated. Essentially this occurred because, with his call to be an apostle, Paul shifted his allegiance from Pharisaism to faith in Christ, a change which led him historically beyond the religious insights of the Pharisees. It was precisely because Paul had been called as a faithful

Jew to be an apostle of Jesus Christ that he became
more than just a Pharisee.

Paul, as he writes in 2 Cor. 4:6, had been allowed to
behold the glory of God in the face of the crucified
and risen Jesus of Nazareth, and he understood this
glory as the decisive appearance of God's love and
righteousness. When we accept this experience of the
apostle, then his criticism of the exclusive revelatory
claim of the Mosaic law, his rejection of an anthropolo-
gy which does not take the burden of sin seriously, his
hope in an ultimate justification through the interces-
sion of Christ, etc., all appear as the natural consequences of his encounter with Christ. Interestingly
enough, in developing all of these consequences Paul
refers to the Scriptures we Christians have labeled the
Old Testament. Moreover, they are consequences whose
linguistic roots actually reach back into ancient Old
Testament-Jewish traditions. This rootedness, in my
view, is highly significant for Jewish-Christian dialogue.
To this day the Old Testament does not speak to us
with a single voice; thus precisely a person like Paul
forces us all to listen anew to the Old Testament and
to inquire how the Scriptures of the Old Testament
should be interpreted. The question, therefore, is whether they can be rightly understood only by Christians,
only by the synagogue, or indeed only by both together.
At the heart of this question lies the continuing problem of how to present Jesus' mission in the light of
Scripture. This basic question is still open, and it would
be a splendid and great step forward if we could dis-

cuss and debate it anew in a fraternal manner. We would then truly be dealing with our most basic similarities and differences, yet without disowning Paul.

Of equally great significance to the complex of problems we have just touched upon, it seems to me, is the insight that it is historically impossible to transform Paul, the apostle to the Gentiles for Israel's sake, into a mere pioneer of Gentile Christianity, and so to rob him of his Jewish religious roots. Just as Paul became more than a Pharisee through the power of his calling, so he will always be more than a mere Gentile. Paul is a Jew who has been called by God in Christ as an apostle to share Israel's promised messianic deliverance with the Gentiles (1 Cor. 9:19-23). To share in this case means to give the Gentiles access to a saving history that began with the election of the people of Israel, a history which is also capable of sustaining their lives until the final advent of Christ. In my opinion, we Gentile Christians, which we in this country almost without exception are, understand Paul rightly only when we allow the apostle, whom many from the beginning accused of being a Jewish apostate, to lead us back to the initial beginnings of our faith. These beginnings are not only in the cross of Christ, however, but also in the creation of the world through God's word, in the election of Israel, and in the promises given to the patriarchs, Abraham, Isaac, and Jacob.

In his controversial nature Paul remains a challenge for Jews and for Christians. But it is precisely this challenge which we ought to accept. The clearer we see that we both, Jews and (Gentile) Christians alike, can learn from Paul, the greater the challenge becomes. Paul can lead us as Gentile Christians from an uprooted faith to a new recognition of our participation in Israel's history of faith. The same man can become a plea for our Jewish sisters and brothers to reexamine the question of Christ in the light of Scripture. Paul is not far from Jesus with his gospel of justification; indeed, he is extremely close. This gospel is essentially based on the same Old Testament from which Israel, to this very hour, draws all of its strength for its faith. All of this harmonizes so well because, as Paul has already said, God is not only the God of the Jews but also the God of the Gentiles. And since he is God both of the Jews and of the Gentiles he is the One before whom, and for whom all of us live (Rom. 3:29f.).

THE RABBI FROM TARSUS

Pinchas Lapide

In this third decade of Christian-Jewish dialogue Jesus is no longer the central figure in the discussion between church and synagogue. Thanks to the current surge of interest in Jesus within the State of Israel, the Nazarene, long shrouded in silence, is beginning to be acknowledged among his own people and in his own land. With this new recognition the vanguard of Christian theology has gradually, though hesitantly, also begun to take Jesus' Jewishness into account and to draw the conclusions this hardly coincidental reality requires.

Such is not yet the case with Paul. Protestant theology generally maintains a Pauline orientation in order to advance his Christology as a definitive church doctrine. Only a few scholars, such as Günther Bornkamm, admit that Paul is "the most controversial figure in the New Testament" because of the doctrinal edifice which he constructed out of Jewish writings and Gentile treatises, that has burdened the history of Jewish-Christian relationships to this day. Most Jewish attempts to interpret Paul reflect a similar opinion, though, given the pluralistic spirit of Judaism, one can hardly speak of a uniform position. Neither the genius of Paul nor the Jewish gallery of Pauline portraits can be squeezed into the narrow confines of a short essay. But perhaps it is possible to reduce the entire spectrum of Jewish interpretations to a common denominator in this way: Jesus is most often regarded as a God-fearing, though unconventional Jew, while Paul, it is said, in order to create a Gentile church which was free of the law out of a community originally related to the synagogue, turned the faith of Jesus into belief in Christ, and so became an apostate who trod on that which was once holy to him.

1. Toward a New Jewish Portrait of Paul

I believe the time has come to sketch a new Jewish portrait of Paul, more equitable in its characterization of the apostle to the Gentiles and in its assessment of his worldwide mission. But standing in the way of this sketch are the doctrinal opinions of numerous Christian theologians, which, sorry to say, many Jews still take at face value. For example, Günter Klein maintains that Paul has, with his theology, radically profaned and paganized the history of Israel. Ernst Käsemann writes that the actual opponent of the apostle Paul is the pious Jew as such. Ulrich Wilckens maintains that Paul was a Jew, but also unreconcilably opposed to the retention of anything Jewish within Christianity. It must also be said that this same Wilckens considers the anti-Jewish motif in the New Testament "theologically essential for Christianity." Karl Barth's commentary on Romans identifies Jewish piety with religion per se. But the Swiss theologian goes on to equate religion with the most refined form of rebellion and sin against God.

Every Jew who reads such statements can scarcely avoid asking, "Is Paul after all the founder of anti-Semitism? Is he the father of that enmity toward Jews which claims to be Christian? Or might he not even have contracted the malady of Jewish self-hatred?" To answer these disturbing questions we must turn to Paul himself, that is, to his letters which make up approximately one-third of the entire New Testament. If Jesus had provided us only three pages written in his own hand, the major problems of Christology, salvation, and messiahship would more than likely have been resolved so clearly that we would need Paul merely as a supportive witness. However, since the only information we have about Jesus is from a variety of often contradictory tertiary sources, we are dependent upon Paul, the earliest writer, relatively speaking, of the Jesus movement, and unquestionably its most eloquent and brilliant thinker. The Pauline letters—already I must pause for clarification. On the one hand, Paul certainly wrote more letters than those we have received in his name. On the other hand, the question of authenticity has not yet been resolved. We must still ask which letters have actually been written by Paul and which should be attributed to his disciples or assistants as deutero-Pauline. This question is reminiscent of the debate surrounding the criteria involved in determining the authenticity of the gospel accounts and the words of Jesus. Both problems have been so overrun by unproved assumptions and foregone conclusions that one can, precisely expressed, only speak of an argumentation that moves in circles to achieve its preconceived ends. One must predetermine the intended outcome so that on the one hand, Jesus, and on the other, Paul, often appear to be mere receptacles into which every second or third theologian pours his own thoughts.

Jesus was certainly not a theologian in any Western sense of the word, because he was a Jew. Like the prophets before him he gave concrete biblical answers to the pressing questions of daily life—poverty, payment of taxes, feuding between relatives or colleagues, and daily subsistence. He would certainly have detested as arrogant blasphemy any attempt to unravel and neatly systematize the mysteries of God. The same holds true for Paul, the latecomer among Jesus' apostles, whose letters addressed very concrete, contemporary, and local problems and whose style reveals unmistakably rabbinic thought forms and lets Pharisaic dialogue patterns shimmer through. All of his responses, even the most well-reasoned, seem curiously fragmentary, and remain, in truly Jewish manner, open-ended both vertically as well as horizontally—horizontally to an unforeseeable future, and vertically, in that no one on earth can detect or determine God's plans in advance. On three different occasions Paul underscores that all our human knowledge is fragmentary, piecemeal, and blurred, and that all our prophecy remains flawed. And in the evening of his life this Jew, despite all of his self-assurance, knew enough about himself to concede, "Not that I have already obtained this," namely, God's plan of salvation, "but I press on to make it my own" (Phil. 3:12). So Paul was and remains a nondogmatic person whose words were never intended to be weighed on the precise scales of theologians. For me he is primarily an advocate of a Jewish dialectic *(dialektos,* "reasoning by dialogue") and of a Jewish *diogmatic* (from *diokein,* "hunt"; *diogmos,* "pursuit"; *diogma,* "the object of pursuit")—an adept in the unfinished search for truth, of which he was able to grasp but a piece.

It is about this very undogmatic *diogmatist* (truth seeker) that we should speak today, taking into account his fallibility and his imperfection. Unfortunately, his own admission that his life's task was an unfinished symphony did not help him. All of Paul's occasional letters, though they contain personal responses to specific Roman, Galatian, and Corinthian questions raised during the middle of the first century A.D., have been absolutized with complete disregard for their original intent, eternalized and universalized on all five continents by his disciples. Just because a few gossiping women in Corinth could not keep their mouths shut

during the worship service, millions of women throughout the churches of the world must now keep silent.

2. End of the Law—for Whom?

Paul always addresses but a single congregation as
ecclesia [church]; never an institution, and even less an
entire organization. Nevertheless, his responses to par-
ticular congregational situations have become the sacro-
sanct ecclesiological foundation for a universal church.
Paul very wisely admonished the small congregation in
Rome to pay its taxes promptly in order not to provide
the malevolent authorities with another pretext for per-
secuting Christians. Yet as a result of this advice all
longing for freedom on the part of Christians has been
theologically stifled for over 1500 years, the church has
been wedded to the state, and Christians have been
exhorted to a subservience totally inconsistent with the
teachings of Jesus—even when the "emperor" wore a
brown shirt. And because Paul had written, "Christ is
the end of the law" (Rom. 10:4), Jesus, who had
sworn that heaven and earth would pass away before
one iota or dot would pass from the Torah, was recon-
strued as the one who had come to abolish the Torah
which, with his advent, had supposedly lost its validity.
So, in the opinion of the church, all Israel was deprived
of its election, its history, and its future. That in the
second half of the same verse (Rom. 10:4) Paul adds,
"that every one who has faith [believes in Christ] may
be justified," was simply overlooked or ignored. In its

entirety this statement of Paul actually says that the law has come to an end *only* for those who believe in Christ, and even for them only as a modality of justification, or as a way of salvation—a dual restriction which indicates that any absolutizing of the so-called "end of the law" is in error.

If in addition we note that this same Paul includes the *nomothesia,* "the giving of the law," among the gracious gifts of God that belong to Israel even after Easter; that the word *telos* can mean "goal," "conclusion," "completion," "fulfillment," or the "final part" of a thing, not just "end"; that the apostle twice indicates that Jesus lived in accordance with the law throughout his earthly life (Rom. 15:8 and Gal. 4:4); that Paul prescribes a new *halacha* for his young congregations, containing dozens of statutes, regulations, prohibitions, and requirements, some of which seem to be even stricter than the unascetic ordinances of orthodox rabbis—then it is no longer possible to continue talking about the so-called Pauline termination of the law or its validity.

Even more significant is the contrast of Christ and Torah, in which Christ is said to have replaced the Torah as the way of salvation, as Paul writes, "If justification were through the law, then Christ died to no purpose" (Gal. 2:21). Here a faithful Jew can only shake his head in bewilderment. The rabbinate has never even considered the Torah as a way of salvation to God. The Torah is absolutely *not* a means of achieving salvation, for Judaism knows of no such means.

Judaism has been given a way of life for which the Torah is a guideline. If salvation means having the certainty of God's love, then the Torah provides that certainty, for it is rooted in the saving covenant which God has irrevocably established once and for all with all Israel. It is for this very reason that the Torah knows no conditions which would make its continued validity dependent on Jewish actions or intentions, and certainly not on faith, which according to Paul, plays a major role in salvation.

For Paul, conversely, faith includes almost everything. To have faith is to have salvation and grace, life and truth. As he sees it, or so it sometimes seems, one believes for the sake of believing, or as the French would say, *la foi pour la foi*. For Jews the Torah is a gift of grace which flows from the love of God. Accordingly, to believe or not to believe is the free choice of every individual. Certainly faithfulness to the Torah rests solely and completely upon *emuna*—absolute, unquestioning trust in God which summons us to act as co-workers with God in the task of improving this world. But to make Torah and faith dependent upon one another is, as Marquardt of Berlin says, a Gentile law, "for no Gentile can comprehend reality without the fetish of self-awareness." Inasmuch as we Jews consider the Torah as indispensable and, with Paul, as irrevocable, but regard salvation as God's exclusive prerogative, so we Jews are the advocates of "pure grace," perhaps even more than those who have the words *sola gratia* emblazoned on their banners.

When Paul says that neither Jew nor Gentile can achieve salvation by fulfilling the commandments or performing the deeds of the Torah, he is kicking doors that are already wide open to all biblically knowledgeable Jews. It was self-evident to all masters of the Talmud that salvation, or participation in the coming world, as it is called in Hebrew, could be attained only through God's gracious love. "Can mortal man be righteous before God? Can a man be pure before his Maker?" pleads Job (Job 4:17) centuries before Paul. And long before Paul, Psalm 143 responds emphatically, "O Lord, . . . no man living is righteous before thee" (Ps. 143:1-2), not even the most righteous of the Hassidim. That which is and remains decisive is God's Word in Exodus, "I will be gracious to whom I will be gracious, and will show mercy on whom I will show mercy" (Exod. 33:19), a statement with which Paul agrees and which he quotes in Rom. 9:15. To see Judaism as achievement oriented, as reckoning accounts with God instead of counting on God; indeed, to debase divine *instruction* (a concept which linguistically as well as regarding content, corresponds to Torah) by equating it with the narrow-minded word *nomos* (the law)—all of this is an absurd caricature which finds its source in Paul. Sorry to say, it still abounds in theological works and religious books in our day. Torah is the instruction or teaching of God. Quantitatively alone it contains far more promises, fulfillments, ethical guidelines, and salvation history than it does laws, statutes, regulations, and rules, which, it is claimed, lead to "dry legalism."

In the Christian sense of the word, the Hebrew Bible of Jesus, of the early church, and of Paul, consisted above all in *gospel,* the good news of God's love and the freedom given by God to every Jewish person. However, any freedom which *does not* voluntarily submit to law, inevitably leads to anarchy and the enslavement of one's self to the carnal desires and creaturely instincts which continue to reside in every human heart. Paul knew that as well as I do. Perhaps that is why he had so many good things to say about the so-called law. He quotes it about 80 times, never hesitates to appeal to its authority, and retains it as the foundation for his understanding of the world, his Christology, and his doctrine of salvation. He never ceases affirming that "the law is holy," that "the commandment is holy and just and good" (Rom. 7:12) and that "the law is spiritual" (Rom. 7:14). He firmly denies that the law is "sin" (Rom. 7:7) or that it was the law which led him to death (Rom. 7:13). What worked death in me, he declares, was "much rather sin, that sin might be shown to be sin." Sin brought death to me through that which is "good" (the law) in order that it might "through the commandment . . . become sinful beyond measure" (Rom. 7:13). "Do we then overthrow the law by this faith?" he exclaims; and he responds emphatically, "By no means! On the contrary, we uphold the law" (Rom. 3:31), or more precisely, since Paul is thinking in Hebrew, "we establish it."

It is not without cause that the author of 2 Peter complains, "some things in Paul's letters are hard to understand" (2 Peter 3:16), obviously referring to Paul's ambiguous attitude toward divine instruction, evidenced by the contradictions that abound in his 119 *nomos*-references. For example, in 1 Cor. 7:19 he initially asserts, "Neither circumcision counts for anything nor uncircumcision," and then quite unexpectedly adds, "But keeping the commandments of God." Really? Doesn't circumcision belong to the commandments of the Torah (Gen. 17:9-14)? Professor Stuhlmacher is more than likely correct when he calls Paul's interpretation of the law "the most complicated doctrine in Paul's theology," and adds that it is "impossible adequately to summarize the Christological interpretations of the law found in the New Testament." Nevertheless, I believe there is a way out of this predicament. The close relationship between the law and Christ in Paul's letters deserves to be reconsidered in the light of the entire Pauline corpus which has been bequeathed to us. The main reason is the following: God's "holy, just and good" law, as it is called in Romans (Rom. 7:12) has, according to Paul, been given only to the people of Israel. Every attempt by overzealous missionaries to impose this *nomos* on non-Jews is opposed by Paul, and rightly so. In this regard Paul is standing on a well-established Pharisaic tradition, which he also affirms in Romans 4 and Galatians 3, when he stresses with emphasis that God gives his law only if promise and covenant have first been granted. The covenant then is basic and essential to the continued validity of the law. But if there can be no law apart from covenant and promise, it makes no sense to impose it in the name of Jesus upon Gentiles who are "strangers to the covenants of promise" (Eph. 2:12) and as a sort of pedagogical follow-up to their faith in Christ to boot. Moreover, from his earlier activity as a missionary Paul knew quite well that Gentiles were not capable of taking the yoke of faithful obedience to the Torah upon themselves. One need only look to Acts 15 for evidence. Of course all of this applies only to Gentile Christians. For Jews and for Jewish proselytes the Mosaic law, as Paul sees it, retains its full and unaltered validity. He emphatically underscores this in his letter to the Galatians, "I testify again to every man who receives circumcision that he is bound to keep the whole law" (Gal. 5:3). And for surety in his letter to the Romans he amplifies what he has said, "It is not the hearers of the law who are righteous before God, but the doers of the law who will be justified" (Rom. 2:13). And shortly thereafter he confesses, "For I delight in the law of God, in my inmost self" (Rom. 7:22). Mark well, Paul is here speaking of the Torah of God and *not* the "law of Christ," whatever he might have meant by that concept. That sounds just as orthodox as the word in 1 Tim. 1:8, "We know that the law is good, if any one uses it lawfully." I am certain that no contemporary rabbi, even in Jerusalem, would have the slightest cause for disagreement with these words of

Paul. I am equally convinced that all talk of Pauline antinomianism is out of the question.

3. Pauline Ambivalence

Nonetheless, Paul's attitude toward Israel as the people of the Torah was characterized by a peculiar ambiguity. But that is hardly surprising; Paul's faith placed him in a postmessianic situation. The fact that the overwhelming majority of his brethren according to the flesh continued to live premessianically, still awaiting the redeemer, served as a constant challenge to the way he understood himself.

That Paul never allowed this ambiguity to become hatred serves as a brilliant example of his determined self-conquest. To be sure, there is no lack of irony in his writings; they abound in harsh critique and cutting insinuation. But throughout his lifetime his people remained Israel. His Bible was the *Tanak,* his God was the God of his fathers, his Messiah was a Jew, and from Jews alone emerged his mother church to whose authority he voluntarily, though somewhat reluctantly, submitted. Despite all of his Christocentricity, the Israelites remained his beloved brethren and blood relations even after Easter. They continued to be members of the people of God and covenant partners with God, a people to whom the Torah, worship, the *Shekina* of God's presence, and all of the biblical promises, as the eternally valid and irrevocable grace gifts of our Creator, continue to belong (Rom. 9:4 and 11:29). Even though God has temporarily "hardened their hearts" in order to bring salvation to the Gentiles, their final redemption is guaranteed (Rom. 11:26). It is to the Jews that Paul first and finally promises salvation; indeed it often appears as if the entire mission to the Gentiles is only a roundabout way of saving all Israel. Even though this salvation lies in the future, for Paul it is so close at hand that he can speak of the radiance of God's mercy as already shining upon contemporary Israel. To the Gentile Christians in Rome he says, "They [Israel] have *now* been disobedient in order that by the mercy shown you they also *now* receive mercy" (Rom. 11:31). Intensive expectation, an emphatic solidarity with his people, and love for the converted Gentiles here flow together into a powerful certainty of salvation.

Since Paul's time almost 2000 years have passed and the parousia for which he so feverishly longed has not yet taken place. Much has happened in different ways from what he hoped. Yet, even in the sobering retrospection of our generation, the impact of his pervasive faith has waned but little, particularly where questions of soteriology are concerned. It amounts almost to criminal superficiality to attempt to present Paul's Christology in three minutes, but time is our taskmaster.

Out of the anguish of feeling forsaken by God during oppression and affliction emerged the sense of power which evil and sin can exert. Out of this feeling there arose in some marginal Jewish circles the doctrine of original sin which, in dialect with the love of God, sooner or later must have led to the Christology of Paul. So incredibly deep was the inherited guilt of Adam, so great the powerlessness and helplessness of humankind, that the reconciling death of the only begotten Son of God was indispensable to redeem the progeny of Adam from their own inadequacy. Since the primary emphasis of Pauline Christianity thus lies upon human weakness, salvation, conceived of as *redemption,* becomes the key term of the church. It is a redemption that has already happened, one that is no longer in process, that no longer requires any search for it or efforts to attain it. It is given by God and passively received by persons who thereby obtain salvation without having consciously striven or worked for it. Every effort or struggle is utterly senseless, for, as Luther in good Pauline fashion later said, each person like a paralytic, *velut paralyticus,* must await faith and salvation.

Of course Judaism has also experienced the feeling of being forsaken by God. It knows the weakness of the flesh and human despair all too well. For centuries its voices have cried out eloquently from the pages of Genesis, Job, and the Psalms. But the accent is placed differently. For believing Hebrews the image of God inherent in all of his human children is so divinely determined and indestructible, faith in the God-given moral fiber of humankind so rock solid strong, trust in God's plan of salvation so unshakable, that evil and sin are not given the status of independent entities. God wanted neither marionettes nor blind tools for his continuing creation, but active partners and free co-workers—exposed to sin, but not subjected to it or abandoned. In this instance the Jew thinks as Goethe does, "Whoever strives with all his powers can be saved." Aren't the bread and wine that both faiths consecrate in their worship services tangible symbols of this cooperation? God created the wheat; we bake bread with it. God created the grapes; we press wine from them. Just as bread and wine are the harvest of this partnership, so too the entire world is meant to become the mutually continuing work of the Creator and his creatures. Becoming, not being; busy, not resting; actively hoping, not passively enduring! Therefore God created human beings to be free, free to choose between good and evil, curse and blessing, death and life, each day of their earthly existence. And no Paul, no Son of God, no Holy Spirit is able to free them from this personal responsibility which can become their heaven or their hell. If they make the wrong choice, if they sin against God or their fellow human beings, they should and can repent. In Hebrew, to repent is to "return" to God. So the key word in the Jewish teaching about God is reconciliation, which must start with human beings if it is to reach God. Not redemption which comes from above, lightninglike, and unexpectedly, but repentance and contrition which come from below, rising like a wellspring out of the heart towards God. Judaism does not believe in redemption *from* the world the way Paul does, but rather believes *in* this world. Because of its unshakable faith in the ultimate reconcilability of all earthly discord and duality and because of its incorrigible optimism which begins on the very first page of the Bible where six times God pronounces the whole creation "good" and refers to human beings, the bearers of his image as "very good," Judaism reposes its faith in the intrinsic value of God's world.

4. Paul the Jew and His Mission to the Gentiles

Whoever looks at all of Paul's work through Jewish eyes, to make the entire horizon of his letters the touchstone for judging each individual statement, and whoever reads him neither through the eyes of Augustine nor the spectacles of Martin Luther, but wants to read and understand him as a Jew—the way he himself wanted to be understood, as a Jew and a seeker after truth—knows that Paul did not become a Christian, since there were no Christians in those times. Instead Paul remained a Jewish romantic throughout his life; a Jew who believed that by his messianic faith he was deepening and fulfilling his birthright as a Jew. He was a son of Israel, a religious fanatic and a missionary before his Damascus experience and afterward, and remained so until his death on a Roman cross.

He never underwent conversion; instead he pursued a vision of vocation which he intentionally described in words originating from the callings of Jeremiah, Isaiah, and Ezekiel. The word *conversion* occurs but once in the entire New Testament, never in Paul, but notably

in Acts 15:3 where *epistrophe* refers to the conversion
of the Gentiles to the God of Israel. The New Testament knows nothing of a conversion of the Jews in any
ecclesiastical sense. Paul did not establish a new principle of faith or destroy the ancient principle of Torah.
He neither repudiated Judaism, as numerous theologians still maintain, nor was he the founder of Christianity, as Martin Buber assumed. For him the Damascus
road experience was the *kairos* of salvation, the great
turning point in God's plan of salvation, predestined
since Abraham, which was to bring about the reconciliation of Jews and Gentiles. The dawning of the
new age was regarded neither as a breakaway from the
traditions of Israel nor as an invasion into the Gentile
world, and certainly not as the abolition of Torah.
Quite the opposite; it was seen as the long-awaited
manifestation of the universal basic purpose of God's
teaching from Sinai—a worldwide ecumenical fellowship of Jews and believing Gentiles, a "great Israel"
incorporating all God-fearing peoples. The members
of this expanded people of God were to live and work
together without barriers, as much akin to each other
as the love of God which embraces them both.

The bedrock of the entire Hebrew Bible is impreg-
nated with this vision of universal salvation. It is not
by chance that the Great Book begins with the portrayal of a single universe and closes with the vision
of a reunited humanity. Its *leitmotif* is and remains *one*
God, *one* world, and *one* single human family, whom
all Israel has been chosen to serve. "In you all the fami-

lies of the earth shall be blessed" (Gen. 12:3). "By your descendants shall all the nations of the earth bless themselves" (Gen. 22:18). And, "By you and your descendants shall all the families of the earth be blessed" (Gen. 28:14). This is the pledge which was given three times to our fathers, Abraham, Isaac, and Jacob. Since then this world-embracing tradition has not ceased to raise its voice among the people of Israel. The message of the prophets reverberates time and time again in the Talmud, in Midrash, and in the other rabbinic writings: no bearer of God's image is without salvation, and the Jewish people, small, weak, and plain as they are, are held divinely responsible for calling all of their human brothers and sisters to the single lordship of one God—a united states of all humanity, that *basileia* [kingdom] of God which will finally encompass all nations in an undivided worldwide rule of peace and justice. That this gospel of biblical reconciliation, as Stuhlmacher calls it, is the *kerygma* [proclamation] and task of Israel as well as the final goal of world history was as familiar to Paul as it was to his rabbinic colleagues. What made them opponents of this solitary student of the Pharisees was neither the question of what was to happen to the Gentiles, nor who would finally bring about reconciliation, but solely when all of this was to occur. The worldly-wise rabbis scrutinized their Roman-Hellenistic environment with inquisitive eyes and with a sigh of regret they came to the unanimous conclusion: this is not yet the time. Paul, on the other hand, solely on the basis of his astounding

Damascus experience and contrary to the evidence of
his five senses and despite all of the practical experi-
ences of daily life, held fast to his vision that Jesus
Christ was the awaited Messiah, with whom the new
aeon had already broken in. This unshakable faith in
his own conviction was at one and the same time his
greatest strength as well as his weakness. To him the
church owes a debt of gratitude for its Pauline
Christology.

Taking these factors into account we can conclude
that despite Paul and all of his well-intentioned statements, Jesus was not the Messiah of Israel. He did,
however, become the Savior of the Gentile church, the
Redeemer from idolatry and faithlessness, the one who
made it possible for those "having no hope and without God in the world" to become "fellow citizens with
the saints" and "partakers of the promise," as Paul puts
it in Ephesians 2 and 3. No Jew living today doubts that
Jesus has, as the Christ so convincingly proclaimed by
Paul, become the Savior of the Gentile church; nor do
we question the messianic mission of Christendom in
this as yet unredeemed world.

But since Jesus of Nazareth during his entire life on
earth was a pious Jew, and not a Christian—much less
a Paulinist, we Jews ought to be allowed to determine
for ourselves what this rabbi of Galilee means for us.
If the term *Messiah* has remained a Hebrew loanword
in all languages, if messianism remains a Jewish contribution to the theology of hope in all biblical reli-
gions, if messianic expectation belongs to the indis-

pensable central faith of Judaism, one ought finally to grant the synagogue the maturity of finding its own answer to the messianic question.

That Jesus became the Savior of the Gentiles *without* being the Messiah of Israel, is in no way a contradiction, unless we continue to insist that "the manifold wisdom of God" (Eph. 3:10) and his "varied grace" (1 Peter 4:10), as Paul rightly calls them, must be confined to a narrow-minded black-and-white schema which allows for nothing but an either-or. Certainly Pauline Christology *is* one of the ways to God. Israel's way is another. Has the time not come that we give God credit for more imagination than the exclusivity of a single one-way street leading to salvation? The reply which the Jew Paul gives to the arrogance of all salvation-monopolists who believe they have sole claim to the gracious love of God is similar to that of Isaiah. It is his conclusion to Romans 9–11, and serves as a permanent and wholesome damper on all arrogant human wisdom and on the professional self-righteousness of those who claim to know the ways of God:

O the depth of the riches and wisdom and knowledge of God! How unsearchable are his judgments and how inscrutable his ways!
"For who has known the mind of the Lord,
or who has been his counselor?"
"Or who has given a gift to him
that he might be repaid?"
For from him and through him and to him are all things. To him be glory forever. Amen.

(Rom. 11:33-36)

Every time I come to these closing verses of Romans 11 I am moved anew by the humility of this otherwise bold master in the fencing art of dialectical theology. Having explored the mysteries of God's saving plan to the outermost limits of our yearning for understanding, he willingly submits to the limitations of reason and says to himself and to all of us: *Non plus ultra!* Raising his voice in a hymn of praise to the sovereignty of God, he establishes clear limits for all theological speculation: We are allowed to go only so far with our guesswork and theorizing. From this point on we must accept our inability to understand and let God be God in all of his inscrutable sovereignty and unfathomable ways of action. Indeed it takes a great soul openly to admit one's own insignificance. We can only say yea and Amen to this genuine expression of biblical humility.

5. Paul from a Jewish Faith Perspective

From a Jewish perspective the story of Paul, like that of his Lord and Redeemer, is the drama of a tragic failure which has only since his death been turned into the greatest missionary achievement in world history. Rejected three times, by Judaism, by various Gnostic and Gentile cults, as well as by his own mother church in Jerusalem, this cosmopolitan wrestled his way through to global ecumenism, as a result of having vicariously carried out Israel's prophetic task of being "a light to the nations" (Isa. 49:6). Franz Rosenzweig correctly observed that it was not Judaism, but Christianity that carried the Hebrew Bible to the remotest islands in harmony with the prophecy of Isaiah (Isa. 42:6; 49:6; 60:3).

Over the last 1900 years many accusations have been leveled at Paul from Jewish quarters: He quotes the Torah some 80 times merely in order to do away with it; he often contradicts himself in his letters; he invented an un-Jewish affliction—original sin—in order to cure it with an anti-Jewish remedy—a human sacrifice which serves as an atoning death. Moreover, according to his own testimony in 1 Cor. 9:22, he became all things to all people in order to save some; in other words, he was willing to sacrifice valid principles for the sake of propagandistic purposes; he twisted Jesus' faith into faith in Jesus; he transformed the optimistic view of creation recorded in Genesis, which portrays human beings as "good," into a pessimistic Hellenistic view which considers humans by nature too sinful and weak to be worthy of salvation without God's grace; and so on and so forth.

Despite everything, even after almost 2000 years, one thing remains certain beyond any shadow of a doubt. This mystic, fanatic lone wolf achieved what neither Peter nor the prophets nor the Pharisees were able to attain: the spreading of faith in the God of Israel to the four corners of the earth. In the end we have to thank Paul for having made monotheism's conquest of the Western world possible. No secondary considerations, and none of the obvious differences which separate me from Paul, are capable of detracting from or diminishing this forward thrust in the history of salvation which must be valued as *preparatio messianica.*

Who then is this Paul from a Jewish faith perspective? He is neither an anti-Semite nor an anti-Judaist. He is not even an apostate, much less an antinomian— expressions that would have horrified him. In his own way he remained a believing Jew and missionary, but above all else he is a hero of the faith—not of the luke-warm rational *pistis* of the philosophers, but of the incandescent Hebraic *emuna;* a person who in his initial experience of faith perceived the vocational calling to which he dedicated his entire life. This calling has at its heart the prophetic appeal to a twofold reconciliation, that to which Paul refers in 2 Cor. 5:20, "Be reconciled to God," and at the same time the reconciliation between Jews and Gentiles which has its manifesto in Ephesians 2. It is this dual reconciliation which he wants to bring about at all costs.

The fact that it still remains a dream which we are only hesitatingly beginning to approach some 60 generations later is not the fault of the apostle. The fault lies with those who simply parrot his gospel of reconciliation instead of being living examples of its power in this disjointed world. Out of the depth of his faith Paul knew that even the most exalted vision remains virtually ineffective if it is not proclaimed with passionate eloquence. This insight gave him the courage to engage in theological fantasy. Only by becoming "a Jew to the Jews and a Greek to the Greeks" (1 Cor.

9:20f.) could his mission find worldwide acceptance. This tactical approach to salvation was indeed offensive to most rabbis; nevertheless, in view of its integrity, Paul's salvific strategy is beyond reproach. For if it is incumbent upon Israel to lead the world to the *one* God —that is, to "monotheize," not Judaize, humankind— then the Christianizing of millions of Gentiles is a significant, if not redemptively essential, interim station on our pilgrimage to the last days. To have initiated the Gentiles into faith in God, into hope for salvation, and into love of all humanity—this is and remains the undying glory of this pugnacious, passionate Benjaminite from the city of Tarsus in Asia Minor.

PAUL: A RABBI WHO BECAME AN APOSTLE

The Discussion

1. Peter Stuhlmacher

In the course of the daylong discussion among Lapide, the participants in the pastoral conference at
Pforzheim, and me a great many questions were
raised, only some of which I shall be able to deal with
in retrospect.

Naturally the conversation very quickly turned to
Pauline exegesis and use of the Old Testament. In view
of the objections against this exegesis which were also
voiced in this discussion from both the historical-criti-
cal and the Jewish side I find it imperative to call our
attention to three facts:

1. Historically it is rather senseless to accuse Paul of
interpreting the Old Testament Scriptures in a way that

differs from the historical exegesis of today, a method that is obvious to us and also required of us. This accusation, continually repeated even among professional Old and New Testament exegetes, is unhistorical because it disregards the hermeneutic tradition from which the apostle comes and within which he argues.

2. This tradition of interpretation is quite clearly the Jewish; even more precisely, it is the Pharisaic tradition of the first half of the first century, according to our calendar. When one examines the Jewish scriptural interpretation of that time, one can venture the conclusion that methodologically it appears as compelling and as erroneous as Paul's own. Whereas the Pharisaic scribes interpreted the writings of Moses with an eye toward Moses, Paul exegetes them in the spirit of his experience of Christ; however, in both cases the exegetical methods are the same.

3. Paul wrestles with his Jewish fellow believers and adversaries about the true understanding of Torah, the Prophets, and the Writings, and his letters describe in detail how this happened. Some scribes, for example, used Deut. 21:23 to interpret the cross of Christ as God's curse on Jesus. More than likely Paul himself considered this interpretation correct until his conversion. Having been taught a better understanding through his encounter with Christ, Paul reverses this previous exegesis and asserts in Gal. 3:13 that Christ bore the curse of crucifixion vicariously "for us," thereby depriving the law of its power. In view of the tradi-

tional Jewish interpretation of Deut. 21:22ff., which
we can now trace back to the Temple Scroll of Qumran
(col. 64:7ff.), this Pauline exegesis is no less worthy
of discussion than is that of the synagogue. Or in Rom.
9:33, following the typical Pharisaic rule that two passages in which the same key words appear (in our case,
"rock/stone") interpret each other, Paul introduces a
so-called mixed quotation from Isa. 8:14 and 28:16.
However, before accusing Paul of being an abstruse
Christological exegete, one ought to take into account
his adherence to the hermeneutic rules of Hillel, as
well as the fact that also in the Jewish Targum on
Isaiah, Isa. 28:16 is interpreted as a reference to the
coming messianic king, while Isa. 8:14 is interpreted as
referring to the judging and separating action of the
revelatory Word of God rejected by the unbelievers in
Israel. It is clear that Paul interprets both of these prophetic passages Christologically; but it is just as obvious
that on the whole he does not depart from the her-
meneutical practices of his time. Again the interpretation in the Targum and that of Paul are equally debata-
ble and not merely the alleged mistake of the apostle
alone!

Our discussion reached a troublesome point when our
attention was drawn to the engaging book by Rosemary
Ruether, *Faith and Fratricide: The Theological Roots
of Anti-Semitism* (New York: Seabury, 1974). Much
could be said—and not merely negatively—about this
disturbing book. However, insofar as Ruether's interpretation of Paul is concerned (particularly pp. 95-107)

I find the following disconcerting: Ruether describes Paul's position as "unquestionably that of anti-Judaism" (p. 104). I consider this historically erroneous. I am also not convinced that "Paul's theological thinking is governed by a remarkable fusion of Gnostic and apocalyptic dualisms" (p. 101). There are as of yet no sources dating from Paul's time that allow us to speak of gnosis, and apocalyptic influences on Pauline thought are just as strong or as weak as they were within contemporary Pharisaism. And when Ruether finally maintains that Paul's Christological exegesis is erroneous and "would make little sense to any rabbinic Jew" (p. 101), this is, in my opinion, historically an extremely vulnerable judgment. I would have wished that the author had instead penetrated to the core of the Pauline gospel, namely, the Christology of atonement and justification, and from this vantage point determined whether Paul argues for or against Israel, or whether his Christology is tenable in relationship to Jesus. But because Rosemary Ruether considers Jesus historically to be merely a prophet with messianic expectations who, during his last days in Jerusalem, finally appears to have been willing "to identify his role with that of the kingly Messiah" (p. 67) and does not speak of any willingness on Jesus' part to undergo a sacrificial, atoning death on behalf of Israel and the nations, in order to make her point she would actually have had to contradict the central affirmations of the Pauline gospel. Only then would the evidence that Paul's Christological exegesis is in error have been produced.

However, as long as the apostle is criticized for har-
boring anti-Judaistic tendencies without taking into account his situation and his teaching, I consider Paul to
have been misinterpreted and unrefuted. It is particularly interesting to notice how precisely Jesus' own messianic acceptance of vicarious atonement (see as evidence Mark 10:45 and the eucharistic tradition of the
synoptics), the resurrection and reconciliation Christology already known in Jerusalem and Antioch before
Paul (see the references to this tradition in 1 Cor. 15:3-
5; Rom. 3:25ff.; 4:25; 2 Cor. 5:21; among others), and
Paul's own experience of Christ, harmonize in his gospel of justification. Moreover, it should at least also be
mentioned in this regard that the entire New Testament
proclamation of Jesus' death as an atoning event that
occurred "for us" is a classical example of how deeply
the linguistic roots of the New Testament gospel reach
back into the Old Testament. Without the Old Testament the Pauline gospel of Christ becomes incompre-
hensible at its very core and appears to be totally unfounded historically.

During our discussion we also talked about the
strained relationship between Paul and the original
Jerusalem congregation, to which I merely alluded in
my presentation. Several factors account for this strained
relationship which Paul himself mentions in Rom.
15:30ff. Evidently, James the brother of Jesus, as lead-
er of the original Jerusalem congregation, had only be-
latedly attempted to impose the so-called apostolic decree mentioned in Acts 15:28f. in Antioch and in other

mission congregations. Paul does not even mention the decree in his report about the Apostolic Council in Gal. 2:1-10, and must have felt this imposition to be a breach of contract. Other things aggravated the situation: According to Gal. 2:11-14 Barnabas and Peter followed the instructions of James and did not accept Paul's argument with its consequent critique of the law. Since then Paul had conducted the Gentile mission on his own authority; he had to put up with the fact, however, that as a result his Jewish-Christian opponents could henceforth send Barnabas, and above all Peter, into the field against him. This becomes most apparent in the Corinthian letters. And finally, after the Apostolic Council James no longer put a stop to the Jewish-Christian mission which countered Paul's work in Galatia. During the Apostolic Council itself he had restrained the radicals who demanded the circumcision of all baptized Gentiles (Gal. 2:4f. and Acts 15:1, 24); later he obviously no longer did this, leading the so-called Judaizers in Galatia to see themselves as legitimized and authorized by Jerusalem.

In the years after the Apostolic Council substantial differences between Paul and James thus became apparent. One can still sense these differences in the account of Luke in Acts 21:17-26. Under such circumstances the restraint expressed toward the apostle by the Jerusalem congregation becomes a bit more understandable than it seems to be at first glance.

Following this line of thought we moved on somewhat further in our discussion to pursue the question of whether one could not simply judge the attitude of the Jerusalem party as opportunism in a difficult situation. This question should in fact not be dismissed out of hand. If J. Roloff is correct in his view concerning Acts 28:16ff. (as quoted in note 10), then it also should be raised concerning elements within the Roman congregation. The only thing we can grant Paul's critics in Jerusalem and in Rome is that Paul's attitude toward the tradition of the law is not easy to understand. The dialectic of 1 Cor. 9:19-23 is not something everyone can follow. Here Paul claims to conduct his missionary activity neither as a Jew who lives "under the law," nor as a Gentile who lives "outside the law," but as a free apostle who stands "under the law of Christ." The formulation, "Torah of Christ," also appears in Gal. 6:2. But in my opinion one ought not attribute it simply to Pauline rhetoric before considering the fact that Paul apparently bases his theology of the law on the Jesus tradition which was delivered to him by the followers of Stephen and the congregation at Antioch. Jesus himself (for example, in the famous antitheses of the Sermon on the Mount, Matt. 5:21-48) not only critically questioned the motivation of the law of Moses, but also sharpened and increased its demand in a new way in terms of the command to love one's enemies; by contrast the so-called cultic Torah hardly plays a role in this Jesus tradition. Indeed, it is the object of severe criticism in Mark 7:14-23 par. In Paul we again find an analogous position. Given these circumstances it seems more appropriate to me to interpret the phrase, "Torah of Christ," in a precise manner. Paul appeals to the new understanding of the law already established by Jesus and therefore sees the command to love one's neighbor and one's enemy (in Rom. 12:14ff. he quotes from the Sermon on the Mount tradition!) as the summation of the law.

Our conversation in Stein near Pforzheim was a good beginning. It led to a fraternal encounter that contributed another piece to the mutual understanding of Jews and Christians, as urgently needed today as it has ever been. The organizers and their assistants deserve our sincere gratitude, as does Dr. Pinchas Lapide for his willingness to converse with us.

2. Pinchas Lapide

Some of the principal questions directed to me during this lively debate dealt with Paul's tolerance, the basic questions he attempted to answer, his teaching of justification, and last but not least, a consideration of the antitriumphalism that is inherent in his teaching of salvation.

In a famous essay, Ernst Käsemann posed the question of "The Canon of the New Testament and the Unity of the Church." He concluded: "The New Testament canon does not, as such, constitute the foundation of the unity of the church. On the contrary . . . it provides the basis for the multiplicity of the confessions. The variability of the kerygma in the New Testament is an expression of the fact that in primitive

Christianity a wealth of different confessions were already in existence, consistently replacing each other, combining with each other and undergoing mutual delimitation. It is thus quite comprehensible that the confessions which exist today all appeal to the New Testament canon" *(Essays on New Testament Themes,* [Philadelphia: Fortress, 1982], pp. 103f.).

That Paul was conscious of being but one voice in this symphony of contrasting melodies—and by no means the only or the final voice—is evident from the structure of his first letter to the Corinthians, where, as is known, at least four schools of thought ran through the young local church (1 Cor. 1:11-13). To be sure, Paul preaches unity and concord; but he is fully aware of the success which missionaries who represent other Christologies had experienced and were continuing to enjoy in Corinth. So he reminds the Corinthians and himself that such pluralism by no means needs to lead to schism (1 Cor. 11:18f.), as long as everyone keeps in mind the insight that the church is a spiritual reality, an insight of which Israel, in all of its stratification has been, and continues to be, conscious.

Israel is a republic of autocephalous Bible readers, held together by God despite all of its divisions. As long as this basic unity prevails, the pluralism of beliefs is no impediment. Indeed it serves rather as an aid to remind us that God expresses his love in various ways and seems apparently ill-disposed toward all dogmatic uniformity.

The letter to the Hebrews begins with these words,

"In many and various ways God spoke of old . . ."
(1:1). In 1 Peter 4:10 we are told that persons ought
to "minister to each other, as good stewards of the
manifold grace of God," and Ephesians adds, "that . . .
the manifold wisdom of God might now be made
known" (Eph. 3:10). Who would dare to reduce that
which God has revealed to us as multiple and manifold
to obligatory unanimity or dogmatic uniformity?

Even Paul, despite being convinced of the validity
of his truth, was deeply conscious of this God-willed
plurality of interpretive possibilities. What else could
be expected from a student of the Pharisees! There is
absolutely no necessity for him to take pride in theological unanimity or to denounce those who believe differently, as he himself puts it in 1 Cor. 3:5-9. For, as
he says, "We are all God's fellow workers," and just
preceding that, each of us serves "as the Lord assigned
to each" (1 Cor. 3:5).

God himself will separate the theological chaff from
the wheat in his own time or, as the rabbis say, provide
the solution to every riddle in his own time. Paul expresses the same thought in 1 Cor. 4:5, for example.
Indeed, in his tolerance he goes a step further: though
those who preach falsehood and theologize inappropri-
ately will be punished on the last day, even the worst
theologians will still be saved (1 Cor. 3:12-15)—an
effective solace for all of us, as well as for every offensive theologian.

"Therefore do not pronounce judgment before the
time, before the Lord comes," Paul says in 1 Cor. 4:5;

and in Rom. 11:33 he cautions, "How unsearchable are his judgments and how inscrutable his ways!"

Paul even admits that the Christian faith is not for everyone (2 Thess. 3:2) and that matters of belief are not at our disposal nor can they be controlled. He, the brilliant theologian, and his assistants do not wish to "lord it over your faith," he tells the Corinthians (2 Cor. 1:24), but wish merely to "work with you for your joy." This is the true freedom of dialogue about biblical faith, which only in our day seems to get the upper hand.

Perhaps we all ought to learn humility anew from this God-inspired witness to the omnipotence of the Creator. Paul never attempted to assume the role of a medieval pope in order to promulgate allegedly eternal saving truths; nor did he possess the hybris to lay down heavenly formulas for salvation. Rather, he restricted himself entirely to an emphasis on faith, a modest hope, and selfless ministry—three virtues which can still be regarded as the undiminished and undisputed pinnacles of the biblical ethos.

Paul's basic question was not, "How do I find a gracious God?" His conscience was, to put it mildly, extremely robust. It takes a robust conscience to be able to say, "I am not aware of anything against myself" (1 Cor. 4:4). Could you imagine such words crossing Luther's lips? Nor was his primary question, "How are the godless justified?" Unlike Luther, Paul never experienced spiritual bankruptcy, whether in the form of a personal fall into sin or as a "tower experience."

He describes his relationship to the Torah very positively: "I advanced in Judaism beyond many of my own age among my people, so extremely zealous was I for the traditions of my fathers," he said of himself, not without pride (Gal. 1:14; see Phil. 3:5f.). And if I read Gal. 5:11 correctly, he was already a missionary of the Pharisees who sought proselytes for rabbinic Judaism before his Damascus experience.

His principal question after Damascus, as I understand him, was how Jews and Christians, Israel and the Gentile church, should live together within God's plan of salvation. Not against one another, nor side by side, but with one another!

This is the intent of his first answer, which he seeks to support linguistically with no less than 17 "with" words of his own coinage. Jews as well as Christians are fellow citizens, joint heirs, corecipients of salvation, mutual witnesses, companions in the household of God, partners in combat, brothers and sisters, etc. Always it is a coexistence, a peaceful symbiosis which guarantees to both their claim to salvation, without Christians having to become Jews or Jews Christians.

Franz Rosenzweig once said that if one were to sever his Germanness from his being Jewish he would not be able to survive the operation. Paul would certainly have said the same thing about "the two souls" that resided in his breast, one belonging to Athens and the other to Jerusalem—the two great opposing cultural and religious poles which he was determined at all cost to reconcile under God.

With your permission I would like to make another comment on the doctrine of justification which the Reformation held up as "the center of Scripture" or even as "the canon within the canon." In my opinion Paul's primary concern was the unification of that division of humanity which he as a Jew had learned to consider almost a law of nature: Jews and Gentiles.

The provision of a solid theological foundation for the coexistence of both peoples in God's plan of salvation was for him a spiritual necessity which he had inherited from his native diaspora Judaism. In order to quench this thirst for unity he progressively thought his way through to the idea of justification by faith as the Gentile way to the God of Israel.

Since it was as clear to Paul as it was to the rabbis that "all Israel will be saved" (Rom. 11:26; Mishnah Aboth 1:1; Isa. 60:21; Mishnah Sanh. 10:1), his *justificatio impiorum* (justification of the ungodly) is above all else a theologoumenon by means of which he established a soteriological balance between believing Gentiles and (differently) believing Jews. His concern is not for his brothers according to the flesh, who are and remain heirs of the promise, but for those "having no hope and without God in the world" who can now become "fellow citizens with the saints and members of the household of God" (Eph. 2:12ff.).

The basic thought in this regard is that Jews are to uphold "the law" (Rom. 3:31) in their commitment to God's irrevocable covenant (Rom. 9:4; 11:29); Christians, on the other hand, are saved by faith in

Jesus Christ (Rom. 10:9). So Paul, the Torah exegete, understands the matter; but he still awaits this rediscovery by contemporary Christendom.

Since Paul emphasizes the unmerited nature of God's grace as well as the sovereignty of God's saving activity, yet gives equal attention to the soteriological significance of the commandments as God-pleasing works (Rom. 2:13, 25; 1 Cor. 6:9; Gal. 5:21), he cannot be slandered as an antinomian. Rather he, in full accord with the rabbis, should be regarded as an *antimeritist*— one who frowns upon every attempt to build one's own ladder to heaven as antibiblical hybris, yet who is in complete agreement with Rabbi Jesus, when he declares faithfulness to the Torah and the expectation of reward as incompatible: "So you also, when you have done all that is commanded you, say, 'We are unworthy servants; we have only done what was our duty' " (Luke 17:10; compare Mishnah Aboth 2:8).

Much later, under the influence of Augustine and particularly by Martin Luther, an Augustinian monk, the hen was mistaken for the egg; the central point of Pauline thought was displaced, and the doctrine of justification was elevated as the core of the *Evangelium Paulinum*. However, as soon as *sola fides* is monopolized as the sole way of salvation, Judaism, with its faithfulness to Torah, can be denounced as outdated, antiquated irreligion, merely in order to reinforce the very self-righteousness of the Gentile church, against which Paul in Romans 11 so courageously, yet unsuccessfully, launched his offensive.

With this development any further expansion of Pauline thinking concerning Jewish-Christian symbiosis under God became impossible; anti-Judaism gained the upper hand in Christian thought, and the dialogue between Jews and Christians ceased.

Paul, as we know, wrote his letters prior to the destruction of Jerusalem and the widespread dispersion of Israel—two historical events which the post-Pauline church proclaimed with evident spitefulness as the cornerstones of its anti-Jewish theology of retribution. Today we live during the days of the historical-political reconstruction of Israel and the gathering of its scattered people—two events which are also not without some theological relevance and which ought to make it easier to continue the dialogue concerning salvation on a Pauline basis. In fact, pursuing it entirely in accordance with Paul's wishes, we may even be able to move beyond his understanding.

Perhaps we can illustrate the relationship between "faith and works" as it is understood by certain disciples of Paul by means of a parable that tells of three frogs which one day fell into a pail full of milk. "The situation is hopeless," concluded the first frog after some hesitancy. "Besides, I've wanted to get rid of this sinful mortal frog body for a long time!" With this he shrugged his shoulders like all of the good gnostics who had read Paul—and drowned.

"God will surely intervene!" said the second frog. "At long last I shall commit myself to the principle of faith enunciated in Galatians 3—as Paul taught us."

With this the pious Gentile frog peacefully crossed his front legs—and drowned.

The third frog was at his wit's end. He had no idea what he should do: yet a totally illogical confidence filled him with an eagerness for vigorous action. He whispered the "Shema Israel" and kicked about sense-lessly and aimlessly but without ceasing. Eventually the milk became butter and he was able to clamber out of the pail without difficulty. Only when he had reached solid ground did he quickly utter a prayer of thanks—upon which he immediately continued the daily routine of Jewish life.

Paul's view of the resurrection and his theology of the cross also seem important to me. It is not difficult to perceive that his witness to the resurrection in 1 Corinthians 15 is not directed against those who deny the experience of Easter but rather against the trium-phalists for whom "the resurrection is past already," as it says in 2 Tim. 2:18 (see also Justin's *Dialogue with Trypho,* Chapter 80). The reference here, as the con-text implies, is to a gnostically-tinted religious enthusi-asm, which, on the basis of the Johannine passion for realized eschatology, considered itself as already pos-sessing the fullness of salvation. These Gentile Chris-tians, supposing that the new age had already dawned, and feeling that they had arrived at the goal of salva-tion history, claimed that for them all things were now permitted.

On the other hand, Paul knew, as did Mark and Mat-thew, that Jesus had died with the cry of despair from

Psalm 22 on his lips, "My God, my God, why hast thou forsaken me?" His had been a way of suffering, weakness, and deepest humiliation—quite unlike that depicted by John which concludes with the victor's cry, "It is finished!" (John 19:30). Since in his view everything has already been realized, the fourth evangelist can even forego the parousia, for, as Bultmann has shown, in the Johannine view, Easter, Pentecost, and parousia coincide.

As I see it, it is against this *theologia gloriae* that Paul raises his great hymn of hope in Romans 8, nullifying all the exuberance of the *ede gegonen,* the "already happened," with a clear eschatological "not yet." Between the ecstasy of John and the pragmatics of doubt in 2 Peter 3:4, which sees everything as it has been and is unable to discover anything new after Easter, Paul seeks a middle way:

Those who believe already have the Spirit, but only as "the first fruits" (Rom. 8:23).

Christians possess a vast treasure, but provisionally, "in earthen vessels" (2 Cor. 4:7).

They are indeed "children of light," but must for the time being still live in the darkness of this world (1 Thess. 5:5).

They are truly redeemed, but at the moment only in hope (Rom. 8:24), for "hope that is seen is not hope."

So in the end even in his Christology Paul still remains true to his Jewish roots. Salvation continues to be a hope, not something we possess or own.

This view, it seems to me, is very important to the future of Christian-Jewish dialogue. For every form of salvation-triumphalism which sees its conclusive fulfillment in Golgotha must write off the Jews as unbelieving, unsaved, and everlastingly obstinate. Only those who, with Paul, are willing to see in the cross and resurrection a pledge of hope, a promise-filled beginning and who share with all creation the eager longing for complete redemption (Rom. 8:19)—only they can accept the Jews as partners in hope for "the glory that is to be revealed" (Rom. 8:18). For them, as for the rabbis, full salvation remains an eschatological pledge of hope for which we are to wait, to work, and to pray.

According to Paul both the future and the hope of Israel are in a profound sense also the revealed destiny of the church, which has been incorporated into "the Israel of God" (Gal. 6:16).

NOTES

1. See Pinchas Lapide's interesting book, *The Resurrection of Jesus* (Minneapolis: Augsburg, 1983).
2. Pinchas Lapide and Jürgen Moltmann, *Jewish Monotheism and Christian Trinitarian Doctrine* (Philadelphia: Fortress, 1981).
3. Pinchas Lapide and Ulrich Luz, *Der Jude Jesus, Thesen eines Juden—Antworten eines Christen* (Zurich: Benziger, 1979), to be published in English translation by Augsburg.
4. See *Evangelische Information* 24 (June 13, 1979), p. 5: "A vehement Christian-Jewish controversy over the Israeli scholar, Dr. Pinchas Lapide (Frankfurt) was aroused by the article, 'Dialogue with Christianity or Personal Mission?,' published by *Allgemeinen Jüdischen Wochenzeitung* in Düsseldorf. In the article Pnina Nave Levinson, lecturer at Heidelberg University, expressed sharp criticism against Lapide and described him as 'a Christian preacher. . . .'"
5. M. Barth, et al., *Paulus: Apostat oder Apostel? Jüdische*

und christliche Antworten (essays by M. Barth, J. Blank,
J. Bloch, F. Mussner, and R. J. Z. Werblowsky) (Regens-
burg: Pustet, 1977). The volume contains lectures pre-
sented at a conference of the Catholic Academy in Ba-
varia, Jan. 31—Feb. 1, 1976.

6. With M. Hengel, *Acts and the History of Earliest Christianity* (Philadelphia: Fortress, 1979), and J. Roloff, *Kom-
mentar zur Apostelgeschichte* [Das Neue Testament
Deutsch] (Gottingen: Vandenhoeck & Ruprecht, 1981),
I am of the opinion that Acts deserves a new, even posi-
tive critical assessment.

7. For details on these early Christian historical circumstances see M. Hengel, op. cit.

8. One of the main reasons for these floggings might have
been the fact that by this time Paul had table and Lord's
Supper fellowship with Gentile Christians without ob-
serving the Jewish food regulations; see C. K. Barrett,
The Second Epistle to the Corinthians (New York: Har-
per & Row, 1973), pp. 296f.

9. See M. Hengel, op. cit., pp. 103f.: "Characteristically, we
do not hear that he [Paul] was supported during his
trial by the community in Jerusalem. Did they feel com-
promised by his criticism of the law? (Acts 21:21)."

10. J. Roloff, in his article, "Die Paulus-Darstellung des
Lukas," *Evangelische Theologie* 39 (1979), pp. 510-
531, has called to attention the disturbing fact that in
Acts 28:16ff. Luke almost pointedly passes over the Roman congregation in his description of Paul's arrival in
Rome (5:23); Roloff explains this silence by pointing out
that "the Roman congregation apparently did not stand
solidly behind Paul" (p. 524).

11. For more information on this viewpoint see the work of
my student, M. Kettunen, *Der Abfassungszweck des
Römerbriefes* (Helsinki: Suomalainen Tiedeakatemia,
1979).

12. W. Schmithals, *Der Römerbrief als historisches Problem*
(Gutersloh: Guterslöher Verlag, 1975), pp. 69-94.

13. In Aboth 3:14 the following tradition is transmitted as

a saying of Rabbi Akiba (influential between A.D. 110 and 135): "Beloved is man for he was created in the image [of God]; still greater was the love in that it was made known to him that he was created in the image of God, as it is written, 'For in the image of God made he man' (Gen. 1:27). Beloved are Israel for they were called children of God; still greater was the love in that it was made known to them that they were called children of God, as it is written, 'Ye are the children of the Lord your God' (Deut. 14:1). Beloved are Israel, for to them was given the precious instrument; still greater was the love, in that it was made known to them that to them was given the precious instrument by which the world was created, as it is written, 'For I give you good doctrine; forsake ye not my Law' (Prov. 4:2)." (Cited from H. Danby, tr., *The Mishnah* [Oxford: Oxford University Press, 1933], p. 452.)

14. For further details see my essay, "Das Gesetz als Thema biblischer Theologie," ZThK 75 (1978), pp. 251-280.

15. In his contribution to the volume of collected essays already referred to in note 5, M. Barth draws special attention to this relationship. Barth's essay is titled "Das Volk Gottes: Juden und Christen in der Botschaft des Paulus" (op. cit., pp. 45-134).